GREAT CIVILIZATIONS

ANCIENT CHINA

BEYOND THE GREAT WALL

Kathleen W. Deady and Muriel L. Dubois

Fact Finders are published by Capstone Press,
1710 Roe Crest Drive, North Mankato, Minnesota 56003.
www.capstonepub.com

Library of Congress Cataloging-in-Publication Data
Deady, Kathleen W.
 Ancient China : beyond the Great Wall / by Kathleen W. Deady and Muriel L. Dubois.
  p. cm.—(Fact finders. Great civilizations)
 Summary: "Describes ancient China, including its earliest inhabitants, government structure, major
dynasties, and achievements, as well as its lasting influences on the world"—Provided by publisher.
 Includes bibliographical references and index.
 ISBN 978-1-4296-6829-3 (library binding)
 ISBN 978-1-4296-7233-7 (paperback)
 1. China—Civilization—To 221 B.C.—Juvenile literature. 2. China—Civilization—221 B.C.-960 A.D.—
Juvenile literature. I. Dubois, Muriel L. II. Title.
 DS741.65.D433 2012
 931—dc22   2011004239

Editorial Credits
Jennifer Besel, editor; Lori Bye, designer; Wanda Winch, media researcher;
    Eric Manske, production specialist

Photo Credits
Alamy: David Lyons, 11, Lebrecht Music and Arts Photo Library, 15, North Wind Picture Archives, 5,
13, TAO Images Limited/Liu Xiaofeng, 8; The Art Archive: British Library, 19; Art Resource, NY: SEF,
23; The Bridgeman Art Library International: Anna Mitchell Richards Fund/Museum of Fine Arts,
Boston, Massachusetts, USA, 14, Archives Charnet/Bibliotheque Nationale, Paris, France, 16, ©Look
and Learn/Private Collection, 26, Museum of Art & Far Eastern Antiquities, Ulricehamn, Sweden, 9;
Capstone: Mike Taylor, 7, 10, 24; Shutterstock: asliuzunoglu, cover, 1 (bottom left), Feng Yu, 22, Galyna
Andrushko, 27, Gigel-, back cover, Jarno Gonzalez Zarraonandia, cover, 1 (top), John Lock, 28-29
(bottom), Kang Khoon Seang, cover, 1 (middle left), Thirteen, 25, Timur Kulgarin, cover, 1 (bottom
right), urosr, 17, YKh, ancient calligraphy design

Printed in the United States of America in North Mankato, Minnesota.
052012   006741R

TABLE OF CONTENTS

CHAPTER 1

BRINGING CHINA TO THE WORLD

A **caravan** of travelers from India crosses the hot, dry desert. Their camels follow a well-worn path. They are traveling the Silk Road. Hundreds have traveled this path before them. It stretches from the Mediterranean Sea to China. Along the route the travelers trade gold, glass, and other precious items. In return they collect silk, iron, and jade from China.

The travelers have to be on guard, though. Thieves lurk in the narrow mountain passes. If caught unprepared, thieves will steal their camels, money, and costly cargo. Then the travelers will be left in the desert without a way to return home.

But the risk is worth it. If they make it home, they can sell the Chinese treasures in the Middle East and Europe. Goods from China are popular and highly prized.

caravan: a group of people traveling together

Traders traveled together for safety along the Silk Road.

FACT: Traders didn't go the entire way across the Silk Road. A trader would go a certain distance, exchange goods, and then return. The next trader would do the same.

Beyond the Silk Road

The Silk Road was a trade route between the East and West. The route brought China's culture, inventions, and beliefs to the rest of the world.

Ancient China was a time of thinkers and inventors. Rulers governed using ideas taught by **philosophers**. These philosophers described ways people should rule and treat one another.

Today people still use things invented in ancient China. The Chinese developed silk and paper. They also invented the wheelbarrow, kite, and iron plow.

FACT: The Silk Road wasn't one long road. There were several routes from one end to the other. By any route the journey was about 4,350 miles (7,000 kilometers) long.

philosopher: a person who studies wisdom, truth, and ideas

Ancient Chinese raised silkworms and then pulled the silk from the worms' cocoons.

Silk

No one knows for sure when the Chinese began making silk. Legend says the **emperor's** wife found little worms eating mulberry leaves in her garden. A cocoon dropped into her hot tea. When she pulled it out, a long thin thread unwound from the cocoon. She wove the silk threads into beautiful cloth.

After the discovery of silkworms, the Chinese began making silk. The Chinese kept the method of making silk cloth a secret for more than 3,000 years. Silk brought great wealth to China as a major trade item.

emperor: a man who rules a large territory

CHAPTER 2

EARLY CHINA

People lived in China for thousands of years before history was recorded. They roamed the mountains and forests of western China. These **nomads** fished, gathered food, and hunted.

About 8,000 years ago, the nomads began to move out of the mountains. Slowly, they moved east toward the plains. Most settled in river valleys near water. They farmed and raised animals.

These early people settled in many groups. China's rugged land separated them. The two main groups were the Yangshao and the Longshan.

nomad: a person who travels from place to place to find food and water

an eagle statue from a Yangshao artist

a lid from a Yangshao pot

The Yangshao

Around 5000 BC, the Yangshao began farming along the Yellow River in northern China. They grew millet grass, barley, and wheat. The Yangshao raised animals such as chickens and pigs. They built wooden houses. They covered their houses with mud and made roofs of thatched reeds.

The Yangshao civilization reached its peak in about 3000 BC. By then, the Yangshao had spread westward to north-central China.

Confucius, center, taught many students his philosophy about loving others.

Philosophies

Three important philosophies developed in ancient China. People used these philosophies as guides to how they should live.

The philosopher Laozi and his followers practiced Daoism. Laozi and his followers believed they should obey the ways of heaven. They lived simply.

Confucius, another philosopher, believed a good person is one who loves others. He thought leaders should follow the golden rule. This rule says, "What you do not wish for yourself, do not do to others."

Philosopher Han Fei Tzu and his followers believed that people are selfish and evil. They thought people could be taught to be good by strict rulers. This philosophy is called Legalism.

The Longshan

Around 3000 BC, the Longshan civilization developed south and east of the Yangshao. The Longshan built villages at the mouth of the Yangtze River. The Longshan learned that the marshy land was perfect for growing rice.

The Longshan were advanced. They used potter's wheels to create polished black pottery. They baked bricks in ovens and used these bricks to build homes.

a Longshan vase

Around 2400 BC, changes to the Longshan began to take place. More and more people moved to villages. Each village had a leader. As towns grew and became richer, some leaders became more powerful. The most powerful leaders began to rule as kings. When they died, kings passed power to their sons or brothers. This style of family rule is called a **dynasty**.

dynasty: a series of rulers from the same family

CHAPTER 3

DYNASTIES

The Shang Dynasty is the oldest dynasty for which written records have been found. Historians believe a **rebel** leader named Tang defeated the last Longshan ruler in 1700 BC. King Tang of the Shang Dynasty ruled a group of towns in the Yellow River valley.

The Shang made many advances. Around 1500 BC, they discovered how to make bronze. They made weapons and tools from this metal. The Shang learned to carve jade and ivory. Silk weavers invented a loom to make cloth.

Each Shang king guided the people's religious beliefs. The king was thought to be the messenger of the gods.

rebel: someone who fights against a government

The loom made it possible for the ancient Chinese to create large quantities of silk.

Thirty kings ruled during the Shang Dynasty. The last king, Di Xin, was a cruel man. He killed many innocent people. He forced his subjects to pay high taxes. He sent his army to fight in the east. But he left the rest of the kingdom unprotected.

Zhou Dynasty

About 1050 BC, the Zhou invaded from the west and defeated the Shang. They took over the kingdom. The Zhou Dynasty ruled for more than 800 years.

The Zhou kingdom was very large. The king divided the land into more than 200 **city-states**. He chose close friends and family members as rulers of each city.

The king governed by a system called the **Mandate** of Heaven. The people believed the gods expected kings to care for their subjects. As long as a king obeyed the gods, he and his family would remain in command. If the king was overthrown, the gods were not pleased and wanted a new king.

a pot used during the Zhou Dynasty

city-state: a self-governing community including a town and its surrounding territory

mandate: a rule or expectation

an ancient painting of King Mu of Zhou being entertained by a musician

FACT: Confucianism, Daoism, and Legalism all developed during the last part of the Zhou Dynasty.

CHAPTER 4

A UNITED CHINA

In 221 BC, the Qin army defeated the Zhou. After this victory, the Qin conquered other territories. For the first time, all of China was united. The Qin Dynasty ruled from 221 to 206 BC.

The leader of the Qin called himself Qin Shi Huangdi or "First Emperor." The First Emperor was a powerful but cruel leader. He followed the ideas of Legalism and ruled through fear. He burned books containing the ideas of Confucius and other philosophers.

Most citizens feared and hated the Emperor of Qin. He killed those who didn't agree with him. He forced nobles to move to the capital city where he could control them.

an ancient painting on silk showing the Emperor of Qin traveling through the countryside

The Great Wall of China is the longest structure ever built. It is about 5,500 miles (8,851 km) long.

The Great Wall

Earlier people had built walls to keep invaders out of their territories. The Emperor of Qin ordered workers to connect them into one long wall. Later, these connected walls became known as the Great Wall of China.

FACT: Sections of the Great Wall were built to protect traders on the Silk Road from thieves.

Han Dynasty

The people were not happy with Qin's cruel rule. Nobles did not like being forced to live away from their homes.

When the Emperor of Qin died in 210 BC, his son took over the throne. He ruled only a few years. Enemies killed him and fought for control of China. In 206 BC, a leader named Liu Bang defeated the Qin Dynasty.

Liu Bang was the first ruler of the Han Dynasty. The Han Dynasty is separated into Western and Eastern periods because the location of the capital moved from west to east. The Western Han period began in 206 BC and ended in AD 9.

Rulers of the Western Han period were open to new ideas. They kept China united as the Qin had. But the Han emperors did not believe Legalism was the only way to run the government. They allowed the teachings of Confucius to be practiced. Education became very important. Chinese scholars recorded history in books.

a painting of Liu Bang, first ruler of the Han Dynasty

FACT: Arts and sciences were very important during the Han Dynasty. During this time, the ancient Chinese invented paper and an instrument to detect earthquakes.

The Silk Road

In 138 BC, the emperor sent explorer Zhang Qian to explore countries in the west. When he returned 13 years later, the Chinese began building a series of roads. These roads helped connect China to the countries Zhang had visited. Traders sold silk and other goods along the route known as the Silk Road.

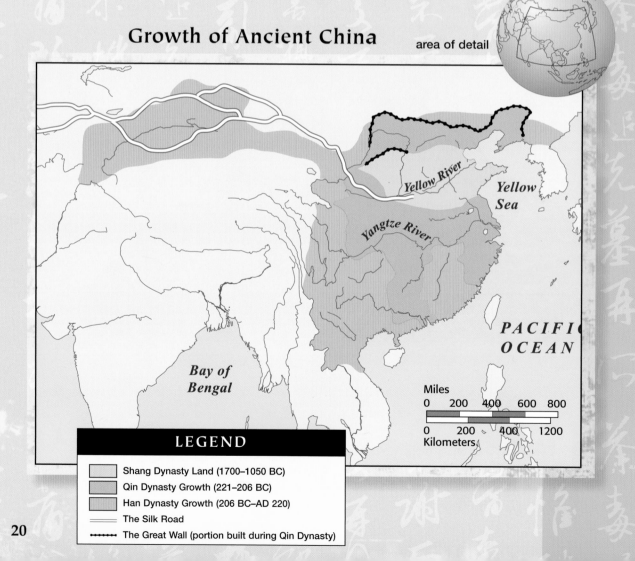

Growth of Ancient China

area of detail

Yellow River

Yellow Sea

Yangtze River

PACIFIC OCEAN

Bay of Bengal

Miles
0   200   400   600   800

0   200   400   1200
Kilometers

LEGEND

Shang Dynasty Land (1700–1050 BC)

Qin Dynasty Growth (221–206 BC)

Han Dynasty Growth (206 BC–AD 220)

The Silk Road

The Great Wall (portion built during Qin Dynasty)

Eastern Han Dynasty

In AD 9, Wang Mang took the throne. He was not a **descendant** of the Han. Wang Mang ruled for only 13 years. He was killed in AD 22. Almost four years later, Liu Hsiu, a member of the Han family, became emperor. The period called the Eastern Han began.

The emperor wanted to expand his territory to the west. In AD 73, the Han emperor sent General Ban Chao to make peace with the western tribes. General Ban Chao's work made the Silk Road safer for travelers.

Troubles arose in the Han Dynasty. Wealthy nobles wanted more power. Peasants wanted freedom from the government. These two groups fought each other. The emperors began to lose control of the empire.

In AD 184, an army of rebels called the Yellow Turbans tried to take power. The emperor's army defeated them. But the Han Dynasty was weakened. By AD 220, China had split into three kingdoms. China would not be united again for nearly 400 years. The Eastern Han Dynasty is considered the last dynasty of ancient China.

descendant: a person's children and family members born after those children

CHAPTER 5

MAJOR ACHIEVEMENTS

The ancient Chinese are known for many inventions. Their ideas about living with respect for others have become models for societies. Much of what they achieved helped change the world.

The Chinese invented a system of writing during the Shang Dynasty. Their letters, called characters, were like tiny pictures. Each character stood for an idea rather than a sound.

The Chinese looked at writing as an art form. They practiced it carefully. The Chinese sometimes practiced writing on wood. To erase their writing, they shaved off the top layer. Then they could write again on the same piece of wood. The Chinese also wrote on bamboo and silk. Around AD 100, the Chinese invented paper.

a sample of Chinese writing

a scene from an ancient vase showing iron workers in China

Bronze and Iron

One of the earliest advances in ancient China was the use of metals. By 1500 BC, the Chinese used bronze to make weapons and tools.

The Chinese were more advanced than the rest of the world in the use of iron. Other civilizations heated iron ore and hammered it into shapes. About 550 BC, the Chinese began melting iron at very high temperatures. They shaped the iron in molds to make tools and weapons that were much stronger.

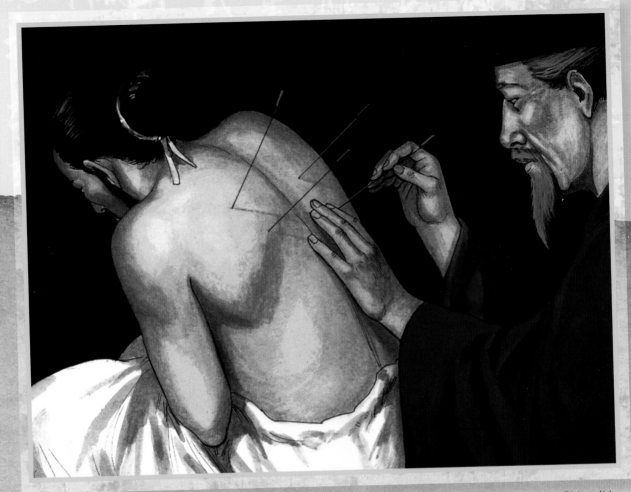

Acupuncture was invented in ancient China. It is still practiced in many places around the world.

Medicine

Ancient Chinese doctors knew many things about the human body. Doctors used healing plants to invent cures for many illnesses.

Doctors treated some illnesses with acupuncture. They placed needles into certain parts of the body. The pressure from the needles relieved problems in other areas of the body.

Inventions

The ancient Chinese were encouraged to question, experiment, and find answers. Many of the inventions they created are still used today. To help carry heavy objects, the ancient Chinese invented the wheelbarrow. They also invented umbrellas, chopsticks, and kites.

Inventions and discoveries continued throughout Chinese history. In later centuries, the Chinese learned how to make gunpowder. They invented fireworks and rockets. They also made the first mechanical clock.

The Chinese gave the world a collection of beautiful arts and crafts. The Chinese invented a special glazed pottery called porcelain. Today this type of pottery is called china.

FACT: The ancient Chinese also invented kid-friendly items, including jump ropes and ice cream.

Astronomy

The ancient Chinese were early astronomers. They kept track of time by watching the movement of the Sun. They used the stars to guide their way at night. The Chinese were some of the earliest people to make maps of the stars.

FACT: The ancient Chinese discovered a comet that returned every 76 years. Today we call it Halley's Comet.

Chinese astronomers took careful notes about what they observed. Those notes helped later astronomers learn about space.

The fireworks used to celebrate occasions today were invented in ancient China.

Lasting Influence

China was among the greatest of ancient civilizations. Its rich history is filled with achievements and traditions. Today people around the world continue to use ancient China's inventions, philosophies, and medicine.

TIMELINE

5000 BC

The Yangshao settle villages along the Yellow River.

1700 BC

The Shang Dynasty takes over rule of China.

221 BC

The Qin Dynasty begins rule of China.

5000   **3000**   **1000**

about 3000 BC

The Longshan form villages around the Yangtze River; the Chinese begin to use a potter's wheel to make pottery.

about 1050 BC

The Zhou defeat the Shang and take over the kingdom.

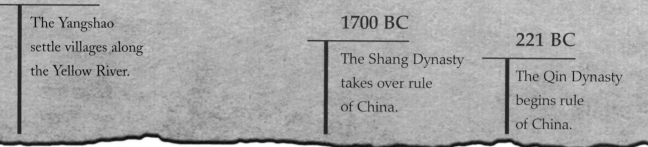

206 BC

The Western Han Dynasty rules China. This dynasty lasts until AD 9.

AD 184

Yellow Turbans try to overthrow the emperor.

200   100   **AD**   100   200

138 BC

Zhang Qian explores the west; his work opens a route called the Silk Road.

AD 25

The Eastern Han Dynasty takes over rule of China.

AD 220

The Han Dynasty ends; China splits into three kingdoms.

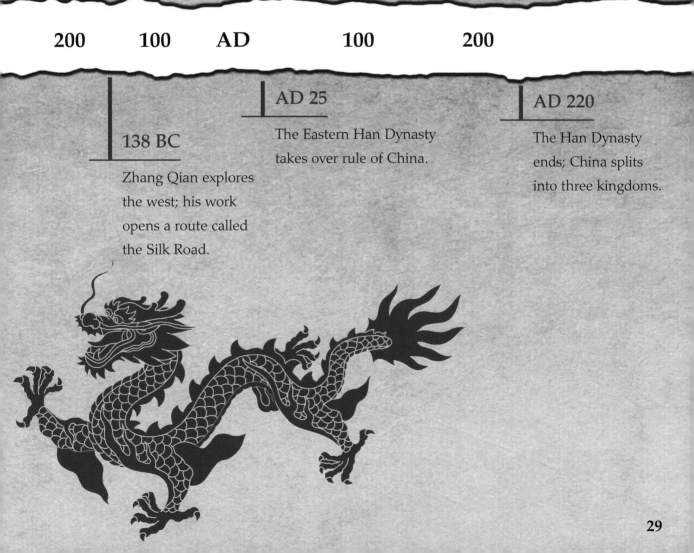

GLOSSARY

caravan (KA-ruh-van)—a group of people or vehicles traveling together

city-state (SI-tee STAYT)—a self-governing community including a town and its surrounding territory

descendant (di-SEN-duhnt)—a person's children and family members born after those children

dynasty (DY-nuh-stee)—a series of rulers from the same family

emperor (EM-puhr-uhr)—a man who rules a large territory

mandate (MAN-dayt)—a rule or expectation

nomad (NOH-mad)—a person who travels from place to place to find food and water

philosopher (fuh-LOSS-uh-fer)—a person who studies wisdom, truth, and ideas

rebel (REB-uhl)—someone who fights against a government or the people in charge of something

READ MORE

Binns, Tristan Boyer. *Ancient Chinese.* Ancient Civilizations. Minneapolis: Compass Point Books, 2007.

Catel, Patrick. *What Did the Ancient Chinese Do For Me?.* Linking the Past and Present. Chicago: Heinemann Library, 2011.

Friedman, Mel. *Ancient China.* A True Book. New York: Children's Press, 2010.

Steele, Philip. *The Chinese Empire.* Passport to the Past. New York: Rosen Pub., 2009.

INTERNET SITES

FactHound offers a safe, fun way to find Internet sites related to this book. All of the sites on FactHound have been researched by our staff.

Here's all you do:

Visit *www.facthound.com*

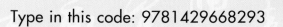

Type in this code: 9781429668293

Super-cool stuff!

Check out projects, games and lots more at
www.capstonekids.com

INDEX